S0-EFO-095

Green
Sea Turtles

Becker, John E., 1942–
Green sea turtles /

c2004.
33305207714019
ca   02/24/05

Returning Wildlife

Green Sea Turtles

John E. Becker

KIDHAVEN
PRESS™

THOMSON

GALE

SANTA CLARA COUNTY LIBRARY

3 3305 20771 4019

San D   veland
New   unich

To my grandson, Ryan.

© 2004 by KidHaven Press. KidHaven Press is an imprint of The Gale Group, Inc., a division of Thomson Learning, Inc.

KidHaven™ and Thomson Learning™ are trademarks used herein under license.

For more information, contact
KidHaven Press
27500 Drake Rd.
Farmington Hills, MI 48331-3535
Or you can visit our Internet site at http://www.gale.com

ALL RIGHTS RESERVED.
No part of this work covered by the copyright hereon may be reproduced or used in any form or by any means—graphic, electronic, or mechanical, including photocopying, recording, taping, Web distribution or information storage retrieval systems—without the written permission of the publisher.

LIBRARY OF CONGRESS CATALOGING-IN-PUBLICATION DATA

Becker, John E., 1942–
   Green sea turtles / by John E. Becker.
     p. cm. — (Returning wildlife)
Summary: Discusses the physical characteristics and behavior of the green sea turtle, threats to its existence, and efforts to protect this endangered species.
   ISBN 0-7377-1831-5 (hardback : alk. paper)
   1. Green turtle—Juvenile literature. [1. Green turtle. 2. Turtles. 3. Endangered species.] I. Title. II. Series.
   QL666.C536B43 2004
   597.92'8—dc22
                                       2003015261

Printed in the United States of America

Contents

chapter 1

Oceangoing Turtles

Green sea turtles have lived in the waters and nested on the beaches of Florida and Hawaii for thousands of years. Natives considered sea turtles a source of food, but green sea turtles seriously declined in numbers only after European sailors discovered them in the sixteenth century.

For the next five hundred years green sea turtles were hunted continuously, and their populations gradually declined as one nesting colony after another disappeared. By the middle of the twentieth century green sea turtles were gone from much of their former range in the Americas.

In the 1970s green sea turtles were listed as endangered in the United States. When legal protection gave them relief from hunting, they began to recover. The recovery process has been slow, however, and scientists are watching green sea turtles closely.

Ancient Reptiles

Turtles have been on the earth for at least 200 million years. They are reptiles and first roamed the earth during the time when huge reptiles, the dinosaurs, ruled the world. Sea turtles first appeared about 150 million years ago. Those turtles, some of which were gigantic in size, adapted to life in the sea. Paddle-shaped front flippers allowed them to be powerful swimmers. Since they do not need the protection of pulling their heads into their shells, sea turtles cannot retract their heads like land turtles.

Today seven species of sea turtles exist in the world, and six of those—leatherback, loggerhead, Kemp's ridley, hawksbill, olive ridley, and green sea turtles—can be found in the waters of the United States.

Green Sea Turtle Characteristics

Green sea turtles get their name from the greenish color of their body fat. Olive brown or black on the top, their shells are pale yellow underneath. Those colors make it difficult for predators swimming above to see them against the dark of the ocean below and equally difficult to see them from beneath against the light-colored sky above. Rarely, an albino, or all-white, green sea turtle will be found.

Medium-sized to large compared to other sea turtles, green sea turtles generally grow to be more than three feet in length (the length of a yardstick) and weigh approximately 350 pounds.

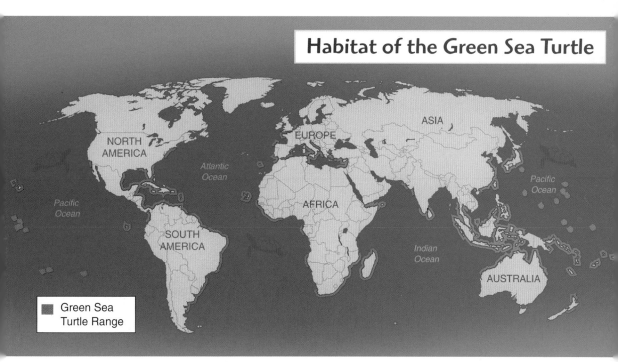

Habitat of the Green Sea Turtle

Green Sea Turtle Range

A female green sea turtle swims swiftly through the tropical waters of Hawaii.

Two large scales on the front of a green sea turtle's head help people to tell them apart from other species of sea turtles. Green sea turtles are **streamlined** in shape like other sea turtles. Their unique shape allows them to swim swiftly through the water.

Good eyesight below the surface of the water is extremely important to green sea turtles, allowing them to locate the plants that make up their diet. Being able to see well may also help female green sea turtles find their way back to their nesting beaches by following underwater structures such as coral reefs. Female sea turtles may travel hundreds or even thousands of miles of open water, but they somehow manage to locate their nesting beaches so they can lay their eggs.

Sea turtles' amazing ability to locate their nesting beaches has marveled scientists for many years. How they are able to travel such great distances and find the exact same beach that they left as **hatchlings** many years before still baffles scientists. The latest scientific evidence indicates that sea turtles have an internal magnetic detector, which some other animals may have as well, that allows them to sense small changes in the earth's magnetic field. The sea turtles use this information to navigate in the open ocean the same way that people navigate using a compass.

Another factor in locating nesting beaches may be the green sea turtle's excellent sense of smell. Some scientists believe that the distinctive smell of a nesting beach may draw the female turtles from far out in the ocean.

Green sea turtles use their excellent eyesight to help them find their way back to their nesting beaches year after year.

Behaviors

Green sea turtles are very comfortable in the sea. Male green sea turtles rarely venture on land after they hatch from their eggs. When females come onto nesting beaches to lay their eggs, they are slow and awkward like other turtles on land.

When sea turtles are underwater they must come to the surface to breathe air, but they have some special abilities that allow them to stay submerged for long periods of time. When a sea turtle comes to the surface to take a breath, it can replace the air in its lungs quickly by exhaling and inhaling in one to three seconds. While they usually stay submerged for only four to five minutes at a time, sea turtles can sleep or rest underwater for a half hour or more. During rest, sea turtles use much less oxygen.

Adult green sea turtles are the only sea turtles that primarily eat plants. They specialize in eating sea grasses and **algae**. Green sea turtles regularly feed on sea grass beds that are found throughout tropical waters.

Reproduction

Green sea turtles reach breeding age quite late compared to other animals. Scientists believe that green sea turtles may be twenty to fifty years old before they begin breeding. Sea turtles breed in the water. At least some of the turtles' breeding activity takes place in the water near the nesting beaches, as males and females gather after their long travels. A female sea turtle may breed with several males before laying her eggs on the beach.

In the continental United States almost all green sea turtles nest in Florida. The nesting season in Florida generally runs from June to September. During that time females come ashore, dig their nests in the sand, and deposit more than one hundred eggs in the nest. Once all of her eggs are successfully deposited, the mother sea

Green sea turtle hatchlings make the very dangerous journey to the sea.

turtle covers the nest with sand, crawls back to the sea, and swims away. She may repeat this procedure three to five times throughout the nesting season. Two or three years later, the female will return to the same beach to deposit her eggs once again.

Approximately sixty days after the female sea turtle has laid her eggs, the tiny sea turtle hatchlings break out of their shells, climb up through the sand, and scurry down the beach to the sea. The journey from the nest to the sea is usually made under the cover of darkness. If the young turtles can survive the predators that await them on the beach and in the water, they may live for many years. Growth rates vary, but most sea turtles mature slowly and have a long life span (fifty years or more) in their natural habitat.

Humans have done much to affect sea turtles. Pollution, hunting, and destruction of nesting beaches have all contributed to their endangerment.

Habitat

The natural habitat of green sea turtles includes the open waters of the world and nesting beaches on which females lay their eggs.

Since European settlers first arrived in the New World humans have greatly changed sea turtle habitat. Many green sea turtle nesting beaches have been lost to erosion, but people have also built homes, hotels, and recreation areas on the beaches that once were used for nesting. When people build concrete walls to prevent erosion, those walls prevent female sea turtles from reaching their nesting beaches and laying their eggs. People also destroy sea grass beds through building and pollution. Habitat loss has been one important factor in the decline of green sea turtles.

chapter 2

A Tasty Dish

Sea turtle eggs and hatchlings are taken in great numbers by a wide variety of animal predators. When humans also take large numbers of eggs and juvenile and adult sea turtles for food, sea turtle populations decline to dangerously low levels.

Raccoons, crabs, ants, foxes, coyotes, armadillos, and **feral** hogs raid sea turtle nests. Birds, feral cats, and many other predators also eat hatchlings before they can scurry into the sea. Once in the water, hatchlings are also preyed upon by fish waiting for them in the surf. It is estimated that out of one thousand to ten thousand eggs, only one sea turtle will survive to become an adult. Even with this high rate of loss, however, sea turtle populations remained stable until European sailors began taking the turtles back to Europe after their long ocean voyages.

Sea Turtles and People

In the Americas and around the world, people have collected turtle eggs and eaten turtle meat for centuries. When Christopher Columbus made his last voyage to the New World in 1503, he reported seeing thousands of sea turtles in the water and on the beaches of the lands that he discovered.

In the years that followed Columbus's exploration, many ships sailed the waters off the coast of Florida and throughout the Caribbean Sea. Those ships carried natural resources found in the Americas back to Europe. Sea turtles were collected along with other treasures. Sailors discovered that sea turtle meat provided a tasty food

A seagull eats a green sea turtle hatchling. Few turtle hatchlings survive to become adults.

source for their long voyages. Green sea turtle meat was especially popular because green sea turtles eat only plants, which gives their meat a sweet taste. The sailors also found that sea turtles could be easily captured alive, turned onto their backs on the deck of a ship, and eaten whenever a fresh supply of meat was needed during the voyage.

Before long the ships of many countries were sailing for home carrying sea turtles to satisfy a growing taste for their meat. Another popular item was "green turtle soup," which was made from the fat of green sea turtles. The demand for this delicacy caused green sea turtle populations to drop sharply. Not only were sea turtles enjoyable to eat, but the oil extracted from the sea turtles was used for cooking, to fuel lamps, and as a lubricant in various machines.

During the seventeenth and eighteenth centuries, sea turtles were hunted relentlessly. By the early 1700s, green sea turtles were already disappearing from many areas where they had once been abundant. Many nesting areas for sea turtles were destroyed during this period including those in Bermuda, the Bahamas and other islands, and the coastal areas of many Central and South American countries. By 1800, one of the most famous green sea turtle **rookeries** in the Cayman Islands had been destroyed.

Cooks on a ship prepare a green sea turtle. Green sea turtle meat and soup were very popular dishes.

When steam power began to be used in ships during the nineteenth century, the travel time from the Americas to Europe was shortened considerably. Consequently, more turtles could be shipped alive from the Caribbean region and many more turtles captured and exported. Few records from that period survive, but approximately fifteen thousand sea turtles per year were taken from the Caribbean region to England in the late 1800s. Exporting sea turtles from the Americas to other countries became a big business. Therefore, to contain the turtles awaiting export, large water-filled corrals were built in Key West, Florida. For many years Key West was a center of trade for sea turtles.

Green Sea Turtle Populations Decline Further

During the 1800s professional hunters hunted sea turtles to supply a growing demand for turtle meat and other products. Sea turtle meat was a popular item in European restaurants, and sea turtle shells and other parts were sold as trinkets. Hunters killed both nesting females and young turtles by the thousands. Even though **commercial hunting** greatly reduced their populations, green sea turtles could still be found in the waters of both the Atlantic and Gulf coasts of Florida in the late 1800s. By that time eight of the original ten known breeding populations of green sea turtles had been destroyed.

The hunting of sea turtles continued well into the twentieth century, although increasingly smaller numbers of turtles were found. By the middle of the twentieth century, green sea turtles had nearly disappeared in the waters off Florida and throughout the Caribbean Sea. Key West and other processing centers, however, continued to process the dwindling supply of turtles. The only large nesting areas in the United States at that time

Green sea turtle populations continue to decline because the laws protecting them are difficult to enforce.

for green sea turtles were in the Florida Keys and the Cape Sable region of Florida.

For many years fishing boats, especially shrimp **trawlers**, took large numbers of sea turtles. Many sea turtles that are caught in fishing nets drown when they are trapped underwater. In the 1980s it was estimated that as many as forty-five thousand sea turtles were caught in fishing nets each year. Of that number approximately eleven thousand died each year. The rising number of deaths from commercial fishing operations combined with the loss of nesting beaches caused sea turtle populations to continue to fall.

Laws Are Poorly Enforced in Other Countries

Early laws aimed at protecting sea turtles were poorly enforced. But once stronger laws were passed, late in the

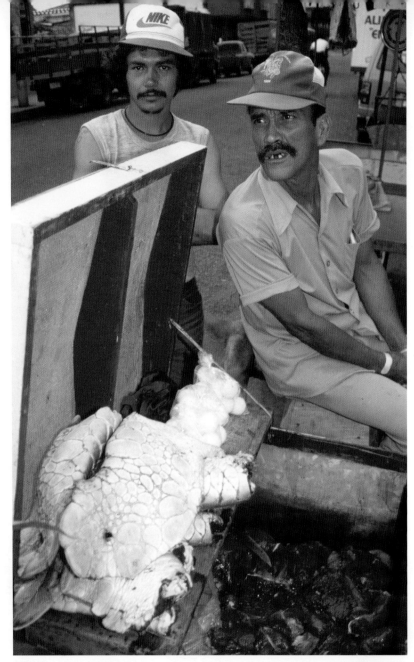

Two men illegally sell green sea turtle meat and eggs in Costa Rica.

twentieth century, the poaching of sea turtles and their eggs all but ended in the continental United States. Unfortunately, other countries were not as quick to enforce similar laws. Because sea turtles travel great distances, their protection is an international issue. Sea turtles that

18

are poached in other countries, or caught by foreign fishing fleets, will not live to reach their nesting beaches in the United States. Therefore, despite the strong efforts of the United States to restore green sea turtles, their numbers continued to decline in other countries.

Lighting Problem for Sea Turtles

As human populations continued to increase in Florida and Hawaii late in the twentieth century, beach lighting became another growing problem for sea turtles. Female sea turtles may be discouraged from coming onto a beach to nest if lights are on the beach. Beach lighting may also confuse hatchlings when they leave their nests. Scientists believe that the lighter, open horizon over the water helps to attract hatchlings out to sea after they emerge from their nests at night. Many nesting beaches have been heavily developed with homes, apartments, and hotels. Those buildings are generally well lit after dark. The bright lights may attract hatchlings and cause them to head away from the water and toward certain death. Some of the hatchlings may wander onto roadways and be run over by cars, while ghost crabs or other animals may eat other hatchlings that head away from the water. Some other hatchlings may wander in the wrong direction, dry out, and die before they can find their way to the water. Beachfront lighting, therefore, became a major contributing factor in the loss of young sea turtles.

Desperate Situation

The decline of green sea turtles during the twentieth century was so extensive that many people feared that they would become extinct in the United States. Some scientists believe that green sea turtle populations had declined by 99 percent. While some people feared that green sea turtles would never recover, others were determined to try to restore them.

chapter 3

Green Sea Turtle Recovery

The rain stopped, and the moonlight gave a gray glow to the beach. As the eyes of the people standing on the shore became accustomed to the half-light, they could make out a large form coming out of the water.

A female sea turtle! Up the beach she lumbered. Because of her large size, the turtle could pull herself only a few steps before she collapsed in the sand for a brief rest.

She came near and then slowly turned herself until she faced the ocean. She used her large flippers to dig a deep hole beneath herself. When she finished digging, she began dropping her eggs into the hole.

One . . . two . . . three . . . white eggs the size of Ping-Pong balls fell into the hole. Then she dropped more and more. In the moonlight large tears glistened in her eyes to wash away the irritating sand.

After she completed dropping her eggs, the sea turtle pushed the sand back into the hole. When it was filled, she rocked back and forth to hide the spot from predators. Then she slowly made her way back to the sea.

She was not there when her babies emerged from their eggs eight weeks later. But she had played her part in producing another generation of sea turtles that someday will return to the same beach.

Efforts to Protect Sea Turtles

Early in the seventeenth century some people began to recognize that sea turtles were disappearing from the Caribbean area. In 1620 the Bermuda Assembly passed a law to prevent fishermen from destroying the turtles that nested on that island. Unfortunately, that law, and others that were passed to protect sea turtles, was not enforced. Sea turtle populations continued to decline until late in the twentieth century.

In 1978 green sea turtles were listed under the Endangered Species Act (ESA) in the United States. The largest nesting colony of green sea turtles in Florida was listed as endangered, while those found in other parts of the country were listed as threatened. ESA makes it illegal to harm, sell, or import turtles, or to move turtles and their products between states or to foreign countries. It also forbids digging up turtle eggs or bringing turtle products into the United States from other countries.

A green sea turtle emerges on a Hawaiian beach to lay her eggs. It is against the law to disturb green sea turtle eggs in the United States.

Because green sea turtles are found in the waters and on the beaches of the United States, their protection is assigned to two separate federal agencies. The National Marine Fisheries Service is responsible for sea turtles in the water, and the U.S. Fish and Wildlife Service (FWS) is responsible for sea turtles on land. State agencies, such as the Florida Fish and Wildlife Conservation Commission, also work in cooperation with federal agencies to protect sea turtles.

A number of international laws have been passed to protect sea turtles. Because sea turtles swim in the waters of many countries, international laws are extremely important to sea turtle survival. An international agreement, the Convention on International Trade in Endangered

A U.S. Fish and Wildlife Service agent holds a green sea turtle so it can be measured and tagged.

Two shrimp fishermen display a device in their net that keeps turtles out of their catch.

Species of Wild Fauna and Flora (CITES), governs the trade in sea turtles and their products between countries. CITES included green sea turtles on their list of protected species in 1975. Unfortunately, some countries in Asia continue to trade in sea turtle products, in violation of the agreement.

Turtle Excluder Devices

In 1989 the U.S. government passed a law that requires shrimp boats larger than a certain size that operate in the waters from Texas to North Carolina to use "turtle excluder devices" (TEDs). TEDs are simple devices that prevent sea turtles from being caught and drowned in shrimp nets. Until these devices were required by the federal government, drowning in shrimp nets was a major cause of green sea turtle deaths in U.S. waters.

Archie Carr tags a green sea turtle to trace its movements. Carr pioneered animal tracking techniques that are still used today.

Archie Carr

Dr. Archie Carr, a biology professor at the University of Florida, was the first person to study sea turtles extensively. His research brought the urgent need for sea turtle conservation to the attention of people around the world. He studied sea turtles in Florida, Costa Rica, and other areas. He began **tagging** green sea turtles at Tortuguero in Costa Rica and pioneered the use of **radio-tracking** techniques that are still used to follow sea turtle movements today. For more than thirty years, Carr worked tirelessly for the protection of sea turtles until his death in 1987.

Carr also helped establish the Caribbean Conservation Corporation (CCC), which has played a major role in the conservation of sea turtles throughout the Caribbean region. CCC helped establish the Archie Carr National Wildlife Refuge and continues the sea turtle research that Archie Carr began in Florida, Costa Rica, Bermuda, and Panama.

The Archie Carr National Wildlife Refuge

In 1989 the U.S. Congress established the Archie Carr National Wildlife Refuge on the east coast of Florida, with the first refuge property acquired two years later. The refuge covers more than twenty miles of excellent nesting-beach habitat for green, loggerhead, and leatherback sea turtles. FWS, the state of Florida, Brevard and Indian River Counties, and the Richard King Mellon Foundation have all contributed money to purchase land within the refuge boundaries. By 2003 more than $100 million worth of land had been protected and more than nine hundred acres of barrier-island habitat is now conserved by all of the partners. Purchasing more land within the refuge boundaries in the future is extremely important to the survival of sea turtles in the continental United States.

Restoring Green Sea Turtles in Florida

Green sea turtles have made a remarkable comeback on the beaches of the Atlantic coast of Florida. In 2002 an all-time record of 3,247 nests were recorded for green sea turtles. That number is amazing when compared to the handful of green sea turtles that were found when nest counts began in 1982.

A number of colleges and universities in Florida play an important role in sea turtle conservation. The Archie Carr Center for Sea Turtle Research (ACCSTR) on the campus of the University of Florida in Gainesville, Florida, is a leader in research contributing to the conservation of sea turtles. ACCSTR educates future professionals in the field of sea turtle conservation, distributes information about sea turtles, conducts turtle tagging projects, and participates in satellite tracking projects for sea turtles.

The scientific studies conducted by scientists from the University of Central Florida (UCF) have provided a great deal of important information about sea turtles and their behaviors. For more than twenty years, researchers from UCF have studied the sea turtles nesting along Florida's coast and they carefully recorded the changes

A researcher inspects green sea turtle eggs in Florida. Green sea turtle populations in Florida have recovered in recent years.

Green sea turtles on a beach in Hawaii display the numbers researchers painted on their shells to help with recovery efforts.

in nesting activity during that period. The information they have collected has been an important factor in the recovery of green sea turtles.

Green Sea Turtle Recovery in Hawaii

In Hawaii green sea turtles were called *honu*. Native Hawaiians considered *honu* symbols of long life and good fortune. After Europeans came to the islands in the eighteenth century, however, green sea turtles were killed for their meat and were hunted for the next two hundred years. In 1974 the state of Hawaii passed a law to prevent the commercial hunting of sea turtles, and when the ESA added additional legal protection, green sea turtles began to recover.

Today, many female green sea turtles nest on French Frigate Shoals in the Hawaiian Islands. Male green sea turtles also come ashore to bask in the warm sunlight, and the recovery of green sea turtles is considered quite successful.

Promising Results

Green sea turtle populations have increased in the United States over the past twenty years. There are still a number of serious concerns about the long-term future of green sea turtles.

chapter 4

Concerns Remain

The team of FWS biologists drove down the beach looking for sea turtle tracks in the sand. The night before, several sea turtles had come out of the Atlantic Ocean to look for suitable areas where they could lay their eggs.

As the turtle team continued down the beach they stopped to investigate each set of turtle tracks. The first few showed no signs of nesting activity.

Then they came to a set of tracks that looked as if the female sea turtle had come ashore and lingered for a period of time before going back into the water. Digging into the soft sand the biologists suddenly perked up. They had detected eggs beneath the sand and soon uncovered the first few white turtle eggs.

One by one they carefully lifted out the eggs and placed them in a plastic bucket. Altogether, there were more than one hundred eggs in the nest.

The biologists decided to move the eggs because the nest was located too close to the water. At high tide the surf would come in and drown the eggs.

Once all the eggs were collected, the team drove their precious cargo to an area farther down the beach and selected a good, safe spot to redeposit the eggs in the sand.

They dug another hole and carefully placed each egg into the hole. When the eggs were safely deposited, the biologists pushed the sand back over the eggs and patted it down smoothly. Then they placed a wire cage over

A green sea turtle returns to the sea after laying her eggs. Some researchers follow turtle tracks in hopes of finding eggs.

the new nest that will prevent raccoons from reaching the eggs. Raccoons are a danger to sea turtle eggs because they will dig them up and eat them. The wire cage will keep the raccoons away but will allow the hatchlings to leave the nest and go down to the ocean.

Concerns for Green Sea Turtles

Even though green sea turtles have made a remarkable recovery in the United States, their survival is not assured. One serious concern is a type of disease that has been found in a growing number of green sea turtles. The disease, known as **fibropapillomatosis**, was first observed in green sea turtles in the Florida Keys in the 1920s and on the east coast of Florida in 1982. The turtles suffering from this disease have wartlike **tumors** on various parts of their bodies. The tumors are unsightly but may also interfere with a turtle's ability to swim. If they are clustered around the turtle's eyes, the turtle may not be able

The tumor near this green sea turtle's eye may make it difficult for the animal to find food.

to find food. Some turtles with the disease die, but others have recovered. Unfortunately, the number of green sea turtles with the disease has been increasing, especially in lagoons along Florida's coast. Fibropapillomatosis has also been observed in green sea turtles in Hawaii. Some scientists believe that the disease is caused by pollution, but that has not been proven.

Other Threats

Trash that people discard into the water is another concern for sea turtles. Fishing lines, nets, and other fishing-related gear can **entangle** sea turtles, preventing them from swimming properly or coming to the surface to breathe. Thousands of turtles die each year after being trapped in floating trash that has been carelessly discarded by fishermen.

Another growing problem for sea turtles is collisions with boats. As human populations soar in Florida and Hawaii, greater numbers of boats travel the waters where sea turtles swim. While traveling or resting near the surface of the water, sea turtles are at risk of being hit by fast-moving boats. The number of sea turtles with propeller wounds has increased dramatically over the past several years, and this hazard to the health of sea turtles has scientists deeply concerned. The increased use of Jet Skis in sea turtle waters has not yet been investigated, but scientists fear that the noise from these machines and the **harassment** associated with their use could have a serious effect on sea turtles feeding, or attempting to nest. Many people and organizations are helping sea turtles, however.

The Marinelife Center

A number of private conservation organizations have played an important role in sea turtle conservation. One

Volunteers at the Marinelife Center in Juno Beach, Florida, scrub algae from an injured green sea turtle.

of those organizations is the Marinelife Center (MLC) in Juno Beach, Florida. MLC is one of only a handful of facilities in Florida that specialize in **rehabilitating** sick or injured sea turtles. MLC has treated as many as fifteen hundred sea turtles in a single year. MLC educates many people about sea turtles, including more than ten thousand children each year. Turtle Walks, in which children and adults learn about sea turtles by observing them nesting on nearby beaches, involve more than twelve hundred people each year. MLC has a strong focus on research and collects information on the sea turtles that nest on the five and one-half miles of beach near the center. Eleven- to fifteen-year-old students also have the opportunity to train as junior marine biologists at MLC.

A green sea turtle struggles to free itself from a fisherman's net. Many sea turtles die in nets like these.

The Ocean Conservancy

The Ocean Conservancy (formerly known as the Center for Marine Conservation) plays an important role in the conservation of sea turtles. The Ocean Conservancy is concerned with all types of creatures that live in the world's oceans but has made sea turtle preservation a special focus. Educating the public about the threats to sea turtle survival, especially the loss of sea turtles through entanglement, is one way the organization helps sea turtles. The Ocean Conservancy's International Coastal

Cleanup campaign involves children and adults from around the world in beach and waterway cleanup each year. The Ocean Conservancy has worked for fifteen years with the fishing industry to encourage the use of TEDs by shrimp boats in U.S. waters. TEDs have saved thousands of sea turtles that otherwise would have died. The Ocean Conservancy has also helped to establish safe nesting beaches for sea turtles such as those of the Archie Carr National Wildlife Refuge.

Mote Marine Laboratory

Mote Marine Laboratory (MML), located in Sarasota, Florida, was established in 1955 to provide an opportunity for people to learn about the sea. MML has an extensive focus on research of the sea and creatures that live

The Ocean Conservancy works to clean up waterways, making the ocean safe for green sea turtles and other sea creatures.

in the sea. MML also plays an important role in the education of people in Florida and beyond. The Mote Aquarium provides educational programs to more than four hundred thousand visitors each year. Marine-science courses, camp programs, lectures, and other programs allow MML to reach large numbers of people with important information about the need for preserving the world's

Recovery efforts provide hope that someday turtles in the sea will be as safe as this turtle in an aquarium.

oceans. Sea turtles are an important focus for MML, with sea turtle conservation activities that include nest marking, rehabilitation of sick or injured sea turtles, protecting nests from predators, rescuing stranded sea turtles, and tagging sea turtles for tracking projects. MML also allows people to get involved in sea turtle conservation through its Adopt-a-Turtle program for individuals, organizations, and school groups.

A Hopeful Start

Over the past thirty years, much has been done to prevent the disappearance of green sea turtles. The progress that has been made represents a hopeful start to the recovery process. But much work remains to be done before green sea turtles are truly safe. It will take the dedicated efforts of many individuals, private organizations, and government agencies to protect sea turtles and their habitat and ensure that sea turtles continue to survive into the future.

algae: Tiny plants without stems or roots that grow on damp surfaces or in water.

commercial hunting: Hunting animals by professional hunters to supply food or products for commercial markets such as restaurants or the clothing industry.

entanglement: The act of being caught or entwined as with rope.

feral: Domestic animals that have returned to the wild.

fibropapillomatosis: A disease in which wartlike tumors cover the skin of turtles.

harassment: The persistent disturbance of a person or animal.

hatchling: An animal recently hatched from an egg.

migration: To travel from one place to another and back again, usually at times of seasonal changes.

radio tracking: Following the movements of an animal by using radio signals that are given off by a radio-sending device attached to the animal.

rehabilitation: Restoring to a healthy state through medical treatment.

rookery: A breeding place or meeting ground for animals of the same species.

streamlined: Shaped to move through the air or water quickly.

tagging: To attach an identifying plastic or metal tag to an animal to distinguish that animal from others of its species.

trawler: A type of boat used to catch fish by use of a net that is dragged through the water.

tumors: An abnormal growth of cells in an animal.

Books

Patrick Ching, *Sea Turtles of Hawaii.* Honolulu: University of Hawaii Press, 2001. Beautiful illustrations and photographs complement the telling of Hawaii's historical relationship with sea turtles. Ancient history is blended with up-to-date biological information and the story of the decline and recovery of sea turtles in the islands.

Lorraine A. Jay, *Sea Turtles.* Minnetonka, MN: NorthWord Press, 2000. Presents the life cycles, physical characteristics, and behaviors of sea turtles found around the world.

Kathryn Lasky, *Interrupted Journey.* Cambridge, MA: Candlewick Press, 2001.The story of sea turtles' struggles for survival, from cold stranding on Cape Cod beaches to recovery of nesting populations in Mexico.

Frank Staub, *Sea Turtles.* Minneapolis, MN: Lerner, 1995. A basic introduction to sea turtles of the United States. Includes information about the physical characteristics, behaviors, and threats to the survival of the various species.

Periodicals

Christopher Howes, "The Mother Lays Her Eggs: A Children's Story," *Brookfield Zoo Views,* Summer 1999, p. 4.The story of how a mother sea turtle comes out of the ocean, digs a hole with her flippers, and deposits her eggs in the sand to begin a new generation of sea turtles.

Kathy Woolard, "Sea Turtles' Magnetic Personalities," *Eye on Science,* August 15, 2002. Examines the magnetic-sensing ability of sea turtles that allows them to navigate over thousands of miles across the world's oceans and somehow find nesting beaches after their long migrations.

Organizations to Contact

Caribbean Conservation Corporation/Sea Turtle Survival League

4424 Northwest Thirteenth Street, Suite A1
Gainesville, FL 32609
(352) 373-6441
www.cccturtle.org

Research and education organization focused on sea turtle conservation throughout the greater Caribbean basin.

Marinelife Center of Juno Beach

14200 U.S. Highway 1
North Palm Beach, FL 33408
(561) 627-8280
www.marinelife.org

Private conservation organization focused on research on, rehabilitation of, and education about the sea turtles of Florida.

Mote Marine Laboratory

1600 Ken Thompson Parkway
Sarasota, FL 34236
(941) 388-4441
www.mote.org

An independent research and education organization focused on furthering marine science and the conservation of sea turtles through research and rehabilitation activities.

The Ocean Conservancy
1725 DeSales Street, Suite 600
Washington, DC 20036
(202) 429-5609
www.oceanconservancy.org

Utilizing advocacy, research, and education, this private organization works to conserve and restore ocean eco-systems and the marine life associated with the world's oceans.

Website

Turtle Trax (www.turtles.org). An entertaining and educational site filled with good turtle information appropriate for children and adults of all ages.

Video

Sea Turtle Adventures. The National Audubon Society, 1997. The story of sea turtles, their struggles to survive, and the people who are trying to save sea turtles from extinction.

Picture Credits

Cover Photo: ©Bob Krist/CORBIS
© Michael Aw/Lonely Planet Images, 9
© Jonathan Blair/CORBIS, 22
Caribbean Conservation Corporation, 24, 26
© Bob Charlton/Lonely Planet Images, 30
© Phillip Colla/Seapics.com, 31
© CORBIS, 15
COREL Corporation, 36
© Simon Foale/Lonely Planet Images, 8
© John Francis/CORBIS, 27
© Philip Gould/CORBIS, 23
Ryan Haggerty/U.S. Fish and Wildlife Service, 21
© Mitsuake Iwago/Minden Pictures, 14
Chris Jouan, 7
© Anders Rhyman/CORBIS, 17
© Nigel Marsh/Lonely Planet Images, 35
© Doug Perrine/Seapics.com, 11, 34
© Kevin Schafer/CORBIS, 18
© Masa Ushioda/Seapics.com, 33

Acknowledgments

Bill Ahern, Miami-Dade Park and Recreation Department

George H. Balazs, National Marine Fisheries Service

Karen A. Bjorndal, Archie Carr Center
for Sea Turtle Research

Sarah C. Dawsey, U.S. Fish and Wildlife Service

Llewellyn M. Ehrhart, University of Central Florida

David Godfrey, Caribbean Conservation Corporation

Takako Hashimoto, U.S. Fish and Wildlife Service

Jim Hoover, Miami-Dade Park and Recreation Department

Jessica Koelsch, The Ocean Conservancy

Scott Koll, The Nature Conservancy

Theodora Long, Marjory Stoneman
Douglas Biscayne Nature Center

Sandra L. MacPherson, U.S. Fish and Wildlife Service

Joanna Taylor, U.S. Fish and Wildlife Service

Paul Tritaik, U.S. Fish and Wildlife Service

Larry Wood, Marinelife Center of Juno Beach

Dr. John E. Becker writes books and magazine articles about nature and wild animals for children. He graduated from Ohio State University in the field of education. He has been an elementary school teacher, college professor, zoo administrator, and has worked in the field of wildlife conservation with the International Society for Endangered Cats. He currently lives in Delaware, Ohio, and teaches writing at the Thurber Writing Academy. He also enjoys visiting schools and sharing his love of writing with kids. In his spare time, Dr. Becker likes to read, hike in the woods, ice-skate, and play tennis.